To every child   A.M.

Text by Mary Joslin
Illustrations copyright © 2015 Alida Massari
This edition copyright © 2015 Lion Hudson

The right of Alida Massari to be identified as the illustrator of this work has been asserted by her in accordance with the Copyright, Designs and Patents Act 1988.

Published by Lion Children's Books
an imprint of
Lion Hudson plc
Wilkinson House, Jordan Hill Road,
Oxford OX2 8DR, England
www.lionhudson.com/lionchildrens

Paperback ISBN 978 0 7459 6486 7

First edition 2015

A catalogue record for this book is available from the British Library

Printed and bound in Malaysia, November 2014, LH18

The Story of Easter

This is how it happened…

Mary Joslin ILLUSTRATED BY Alida Massari

LION
CHILDREN'S

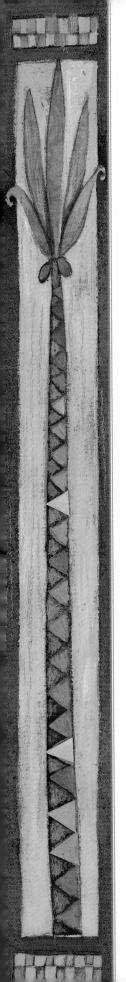

Long ago, near the shores of Lake Galilee, lived a man named Jesus. From boyhood he had learned to be a carpenter; but as a young man he became a preacher.

"Make it your aim to live as God's friends," he told the crowds who gathered to listen to him. "Then you will be part of God's kingdom.

"Love one another, just as God loves you, and forgive one another, just as God forgives you."

Jesus chose twelve good friends to be his disciples and to help spread his message about God's kingdom.

One day, they all set out for the city of Jerusalem.

"It is time to celebrate the festival of Passover," Jesus told them, "and to remember God's promise to guard us and to guide us."

As Jesus rode into the city, the crowds saw him.

"Perhaps he is coming to establish God's kingdom here and now?" they whispered.

They began to cheer and to wave palm branches.

"God bless the king," they cried.

9

When Jesus reached the city, he went to the Temple. The courtyard had become a marketplace for the festival. Jesus was dismayed.

"This is meant to be a place of prayer," he cried. "You have made it a den of thieves."

He overturned the market stalls and drove out all the traders.

The Temple priests and other leaders of the people whispered angrily.

"The man is a troublemaker," they agreed. "We must get rid of him."

In the days that followed, Jesus went to the Temple to preach. His enemies seized their chance to question him.

"You claim to teach people about God," they said. "What is the most important teaching?"

"The greatest commandment is this," replied Jesus: "love the Lord your God with all your heart, with all your soul, with all your mind, and with all your strength.

"And the second is this: love your neighbour as you love yourself."

Jesus' enemies could not fault his answer, but still their anger grew.

Then one of Jesus' own friends turned against him. Judas Iscariot went to Jesus' enemies in secret. For money, he agreed to betray his master.

Now, at the heart of the festival was a shared supper. Jesus asked his disciples to prepare it.

It would have been the custom for a servant to wash their dusty feet as they arrived.

To the disciples' astonishment, Jesus himself took off his cloak, put on an apron, and did the work of a servant.

"Tonight I am giving you a new commandment," he said: "to love and serve one another."

The traditional foods included bread and wine.
    At the meal, Jesus took a piece of bread and said the prayer of thanksgiving. "This is my body, broken for you," he said. "Do this in memory of me."

After supper he took the cup of wine and said, "This cup is God's new and everlasting promise, signed with my own blood. Whenever you drink from it, do so in memory of me." Even as Jesus spoke to his friends of the troubles that lay ahead, Judas slipped away.

After the supper, Jesus and his disciples went to the olive grove known as Gethsemane. Here they planned to spend the night under the stars.

Jesus went off on his own and prayed earnestly to God: "If it is possible, spare me the way of suffering," he said; but he added, "but your will be done."

He returned to his disciples. They had fallen asleep.

A cry rang out… then came a blaze of torches.

Judas Iscariot arrived, leading a group of armed men. The disciples fled as Jesus was arrested and marched away.

Even before they had questioned Jesus, the priests had made up their mind: that Jesus was allowing the people to believe he was God's chosen king and messiah. Such disrespect, they believed, deserved to be punished by death.

All that remained to do was to ask the Roman governor, Pontius Pilate, to sign the warrant.

"This Jesus claims to be our king!" they told Pilate. "That makes him a dangerous rebel."

Pilate did not believe for a moment that Jesus was any threat to the peace. But the crowds outside his residence were demanding Jesus' life. Pilate agreed to his crucifixion.

Jesus was handed over to the guards.

"A king, are you?" they jeered. "Here – a purple robe, Your Majesty, and your royal crown."

They forced a circle of thorns onto his head and gave him a reed to hold as a sceptre before beating him and spitting on him.

Then, forcing a wooden cross onto his shoulders, they led him outside the city walls.

On a hill named Golgotha, Jesus was crucified between two criminals.

Jesus prayed for his tormentors.

"Forgive them, Father," he said. "They don't know what they are doing."

It was around 3 o'clock in the afternoon when Jesus died. As the sun sank lower, a man named Joseph, from Arimathea, went to ask Pilate for the body. Then he arranged for it to be carried to a rock-cut tomb, and the stone door to be rolled shut.

The sun began to set: the sabbath day of rest was beginning.

Early on the Sunday morning, some women went to the tomb.

They took with them the traditional spices with which to prepare the body for its burial.

To their dismay, they found the stone door had been rolled away, and the body gone.

Suddenly, two angels appeared.

"Why are you looking among the dead for someone who is alive?" they asked. "Jesus is not here – God has raised him to life."

In the days that followed, more and more of Jesus'
faithful disciples saw their master alive.

"The work I came to do is now complete," he told them.

"Now I must return to heaven, to prepare a place you.

"And your task is to spread this good news: that because
of my death and resurrection, the way is open for those
who believe in me…

to be part of God's everlasting kingdom."

Other titles from Lion Children's Books

The Easter Story Antonia Jackson & Giuliano Ferri

The First Easter Lois Rock & Sophie Allsopp

Stories of the Saints Margaret McAllister & Alida Massari

Women of the Bible Margaret McAllister & Alida Massari